Simone Biles

CHERRY LAKE PRESS

Published in the United States of America by Cherry Lake Publishing
Ann Arbor, Michigan
www.cherrylakepublishing.com

Reading Adviser: Marla Conn, MS, Ed., Literacy specialist, Read-Ability, Inc.
Book Designer: Jennifer Wahi
Illustrator: Jeff Bane

Photo Credits: Page 5: ©aceshot1/Shutterstock, 5; ©Newscom, 7; ©BUENAFOTO/Shutterstock, 9, 22; ©Leonard Zhukovsky/Shutterstock, 11, 13, 15, 21, 23; ©Pixel-Shot/Shutterstock, 17; ©Adam R. Cole/Wikimedia/Public Domain, 19; Jeff Bane, cover, 1, 6, 10, 14

Library of Congress Cataloging-in-Publication Data

Names: Sarantou, Katlin, author. | Bane, Jeff, 1957- illustrator.
Title: Simone Biles / Katlin Sarantou, Jeff Bane.
Description: Ann Arbor, Michigan : Cherry Lake Publishing, [2020] | Series:
  My itty-bitty bios | Includes index. | Audience: Grades K-1 | Summary:
  "The My Itty-Bitty Bio series are biographies for the earliest readers.
  This book examines the life of Simone Biles in a simple, age-appropriate
  way that will help children develop word recognition and reading skills.
  Includes a table of contents, author biography, timeline, glossary,
  index, and other informative backmatter"-- Provided by publisher.
Identifiers: LCCN 2019034633 (print) | LCCN 2019034634 (ebook) | ISBN
  9781534158771 (hardcover) | ISBN 9781534161078 (paperback) | ISBN
  9781534159921 (pdf) | ISBN 9781534162228 (ebook)
Subjects: LCSH: Biles, Simone, 1997---Juvenile literature. | Women
  gymnasts--United States--Biography--Juvenile literature. | African
  American women athletes--United States--Biography--Juvenile literature.
  | Women Olympic athletes--United States--Biography--Juvenile literature.
Classification: LCC GV460.2.B55 S27 2020 (print) | LCC GV460.2.B55
  (ebook) | DDC 796.44092 [B]--dc23
LC record available at https://lccn.loc.gov/2019034633
LC ebook record available at https://lccn.loc.gov/2019034634

Printed in the United States of America
Corporate Graphics

About the author: Katlin Sarantou grew up in the cornfields of Ohio. She enjoys reading and dreaming of faraway places.

About the illustrator: Jeff Bane and his two business partners own a studio along the American River in Folsom, California, home of the 1849 Gold Rush. When Jeff's not sketching or illustrating for clients, he's either swimming or kayaking in the river to relax.

I was born in Columbus, Ohio.

It was March 14, 1997.

My **siblings** and I were in **foster care**.

We were **adopted** in 2003.

I started **gymnastics** when I was 6.

I liked to jump. I liked to run around.

What do you like to do?

I worked hard. I made it on the
Olympic team.

What's your favorite Olympic sport?

I was part of the "Final Five." This was an Olympic team in 2016.

We won a gold medal.

I've broken records. I am the first woman to successfully land a **triple-double**. This happened in 2019. The move is named after me. It's called Biles II.

I won the most **World Championship** medals in U.S. history.

I also like to help kids. I want kids to be healthy. I want them to have fun.

I work with groups that give back to kids. Some organizations help U.S. foster kids. Others help kids that are sick.

Some think I'm the greatest gymnast of all time. I'm just proud of what I have accomplished.

I want to **inspire** kids. I want them to be active and have fun!

What would you like to ask me?

2003

1990

↑
Born
1997

2016

2090

glossary

adopted (uh-DAHPT-id) legally made the child of someone

foster care (FAWS-tur KAIR) a setting in which a child lives with people who are not their parents for a period of time

gymnastics (jim-NAS-tiks) physical exercises that involve strength and balance and are a sport

inspire (in-SPIRE) to fill someone with a feeling or idea

siblings (SIB-lingz) brothers and sisters

triple-double (TRIP-uhl DUHB-uhl) a special move in gymnastics in which a person does a double backflip with three twists

World Championship (WURLD CHAM-pee-uhn-ship) an event that gymnasts from around the world compete in

index